Critters
CRY too

by Anthony Curcio

ISBN 978-0-692-58732-4

Copyright © 2015 by Anthony Curcio
Published by ICG Books. All rights reserved.

12 11 10 9 8 7 6 5 4 3 2 1
Printed in the USA

Hello! I am doctor Rhymer Roach and I am here to tell you the sadappy* story of when Whateveritwas took over the small land of Zapatos.

It all began with the youngest of critters, a critter named Calvin..."

*In critter talk, "sadappy" means both sad and happy!

Calvin loved to laugh and had very wild hair!

He lived with his family in a place called Zapatos.

**There were nine critters in the Critter family...
including their family pet, Waggly.**

I just love this picture!

The Critter family were a bunch of happy critters
and they loved each other very much.

There wasn't much to do in Zapatos except play Critterball...

I love watching Critterball, but I can hardly see the game from here! I need a better seat...

...and talk.

(Critters love to talk and tell jokes!)

This is much better!

They talked and talked and talked. Critters talk about everything and are very happy most of the time.

Talking is good but right now, I wish they would quit talking so loud! Critters even talk to their pets!

Sometimes, Critters would get what they called madsad* but, since they talked so much, they always worked it out.

*It says here in my notes that "madsad" means a critter is acting mad but is actually just sad. Luckily, I'm here to explain these things!

After dinner, the Critters did what they always did...

Played Critterball.

For the win!

Then the Critters went to sleep.

What?!
All great doctors sleep on the job.

But one day, things changed.

Something new came into the land of Zapatos.

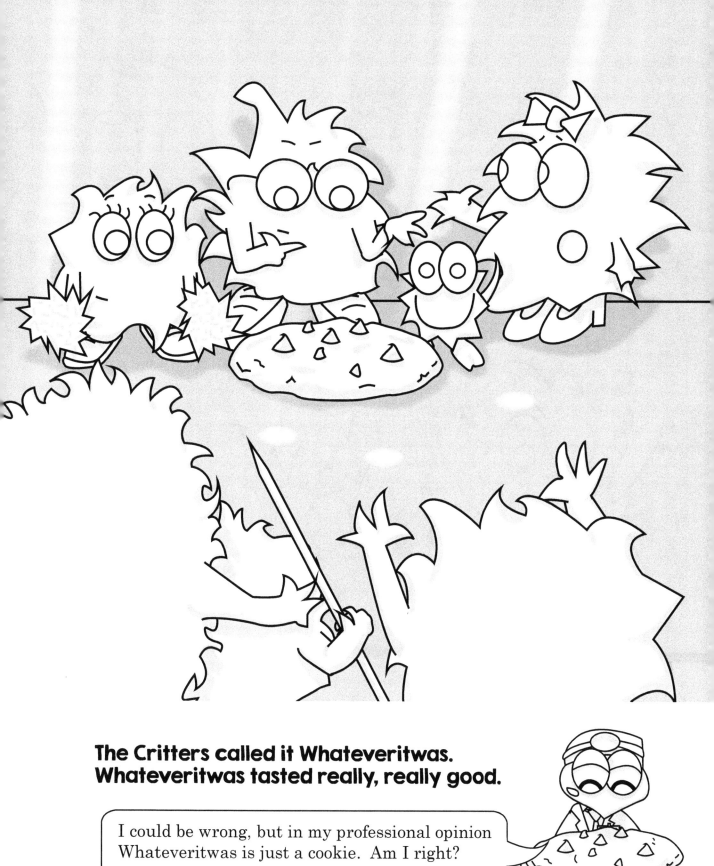

**The Critters called it Whateveritwas.
Whateveritwas tasted really, really good.**

I could be wrong, but in my professional opinion Whateveritwas is just a cookie. Am I right?

Some Critters liked Whateveritwas more than others and some of them liked it too much.

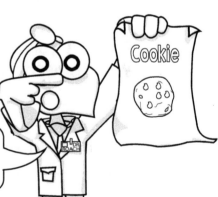

Enough of this crazy Critter talk! Whateveritwas *is* a cookie!

They just wanted more Whateveritwas.

They were happy when they got it and sad when it was gone.
They weren't even acting like Critters anymore.
They didn't even want to play Critterball!

Calvin's dad promised he would play, but he didn't.

Some Critters didn't even want to talk anymore.

They thought Whateveritwas was making them happy
but really it was making everyone madsad.

These critters think they need more of the cookie but the cookie is the very thing that is making them madsad.

This makes no sense! Even to a great Roach doctor like me!

All Calvin's dad wanted to do was wait for more Whateveritwas.

Some of the Critters were very sick, but they just didn't know it.

These critters stopped doing the things they loved to do and didn't think about anything except getting more cookies. This is called addiction. Addiction is a sickness.

Calvin loved his family but he knew this wasn't right.

Some Critters have this addiction thing and some don't.
The ones that do don't want to hurt the critters they love,
but I'm sad because they do.
The only way to get better is to stop eating the cookies,
but just try telling a Critter that!

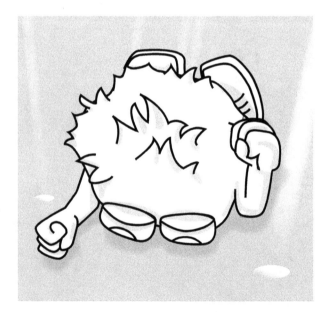

Calvin felt all alone and became really madsad.
It's hard for a critter to talk when they're madsad.

When a critter is madsad it usually means that their feelings are
really hurt and they don't know how to feel better.

Calvin stayed madsad a little while longer but then he talked about how he felt and found out that others felt just like him. He wasn't alone after all.

Even Waggly is madsad!

Calvin wanted the other critters to feel better too,
so he climbed as high as he could to get their attention.

He reached the top of Zapatos where no critter had
ever been.

And discovered something new, something amazing.

I can't look, I'm too scared! That ladder is held together by toothpicks and marshmallows! I have to do something!

Cavlin opened his eyes and what did he see?

He saw Me!

"You are brave, you are strong, you didn't give up!
You climbed all the way up here, you and your pup!

When the pain is inside there is only one way to heal,
You just needed some time and talking about how you feel!

Who am I, you really don't know?
I am the great roach doctor and it's time for my show!"

"Critters here! Critters there!
 May I have your critter attention please!
 Let me introduce to you... Ralph!"

The Critters were shocked, they were stunned.
"Who is this? This doesn't sound like fun."

"Ralph is a dog. Ralph is a lovigood* dog.
Everyone loves Ralph and Ralph loves everyone.
Like all dogs, Ralph also loves chocolate!

But, never, ever feed a dog chocolate! Not even Ralph!
Because...

*"Lovigood" means loving and good in Critter talk.

If they taste it, they will beg for it!

If they get it, they will fight for it!

**If they eat it,
they will get really, really sick.**

**And the next day, they will
beg for it all over again!**

"Critters, I tell you about Ralph because you are no different than he.
Whateveritwas is making you sick, this I hope you will see.

You have to make the choice and be very, very strong,
to say no to something you like, that has been hurting you all along.

Well, after my speech Calvin kept talking!

And a few other Critters decided that they were ready to climb out of Zapatos and away from Whateveritwas.

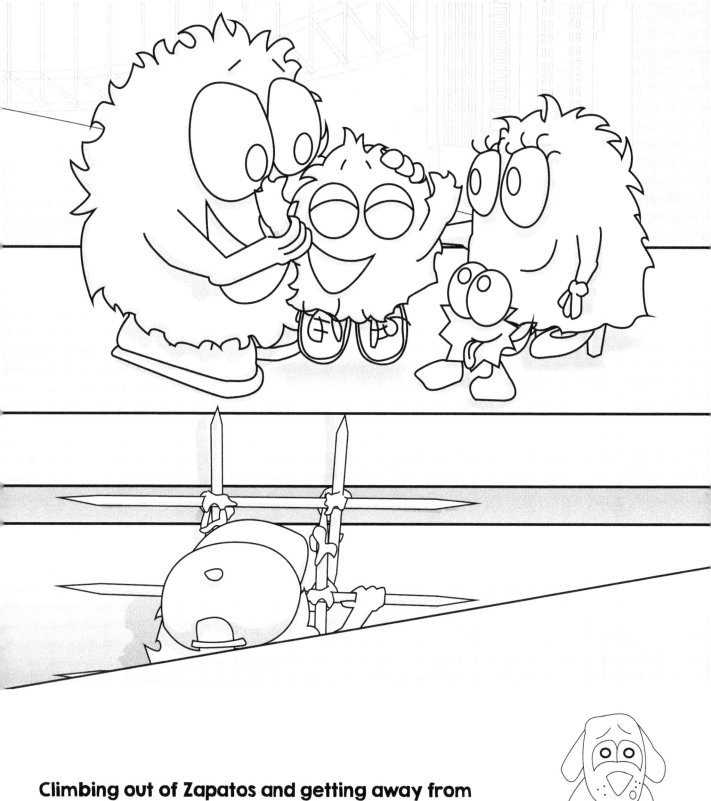

Climbing out of Zapatos and getting away from Whateveritwas, if you are addicted, is not easy to do!

It would be like Ralph (the dog) saying no to chocolate!

Not all of the Critter's have found there way out of Zapatos yet,
but the ones that did found something so amazing, so special and
something that made Calvin so happy...

They found themselves!

LOVING a Critter with AN addiction CAN BE tough

It may feel like you're **being blown this way and that,**

Always bounced around,

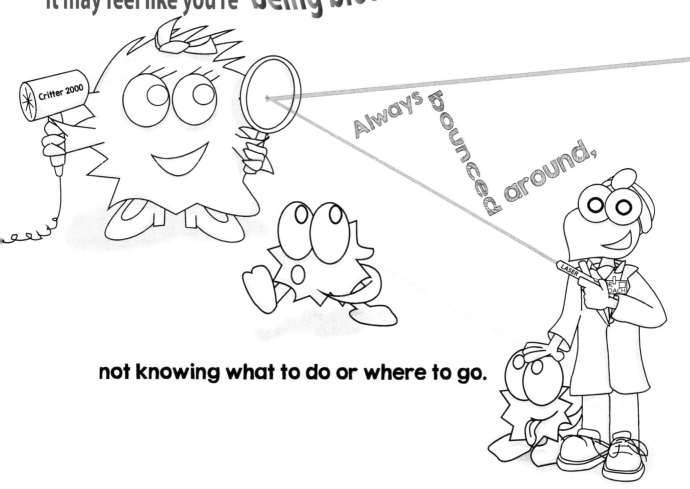

not knowing what to do or where to go.

JUST REMEMBER

KEEP brushing your crazy hair and SMILING in the mirror

Because You're not alone.

Critter keep TALKING

Even if it's too a fluffy dog thing!

CPSIA information can be obtained
at www.ICGtesting.com
Printed in the USA
LVHW101513270921
698838LV00006B/685